THE LAST WAR THAT HAD TO BE FOUGHT

Hammad Junejo

Expressed
Toronto, Ontario

Hammad Junejo / Expressed Books
Toronto, Ontario, Canada
www.expressedbooks.com

The Last War That Had to Be Fought / Hammad Junejo. -- 1st ed.
ISBN: 978-1-9991339-0-0

Cover image: Shutterstock / Canadian soldier is attended by a medic near Falaise, France. A burning overturned German tank is the in rubble nearby, during the Battle of the Falaise Pocket. August 6-17, 1944.
Cover design and interior typeset: Robert Grant Price

For my mother:
for her unparalleled strength and will,
which have always comforted me

For my extraordinarily selfless father:
for the first history book he bought me
when I was a child and for his endless
support and words of wisdom,
which have always guided me

For the faith they placed in me

And for Harry Preston
and all the "average" men and women
of the Canadian Armed Forces who fought in
the last war that had to be fought

In the hopes that their sacrifices
and heroics will never be forgotten

CONTENTS

*"The only thing necessary for the triumph of evil
is for good men to do nothing."*

— Edmund Burke

*"They used to say in the first war, 'If a shell's got your number on
it, you're going to get it.' You're going to die at some point.
You just do your duty."*

— Harry Preston

Introduction

Humans are mortal: our flesh is as grass. This biblical observation is ever with us in peace, and is all too apparent in times of war. The last Canadian veteran of the Great War, John Babcock, died in 2010. From 2014 to 2018, Canada has observed the 100th anniversary of the Great War years with a flood of articles, books, ceremonies, a second great pilgrimage to Vimy Ridge in 2017, and a sombre, heartfelt, deeply symbolic observant Remembrance Day in 2018. But what of the Canadian veterans of the Second World War? The youngest of these (a 17-year-old recruit in 1945) would be 90 years old now. What are their stories?

In February 2018, at Sunnybrook Veterans Centre in Toronto, Hammad Junejo, a historian and writer studying at the University of Toronto, interviewed one of those Canadian Second World War veterans: Harry Preston (1922–2019), a Sergeant in the 3rd Light Anti-Aircraft Regiment.

This book captures Preston's wartime experiences. The reader will see that Preston was not a medal winner or a Hollywood-styled war hero. He was an average soldier who answered Canada's call to end Nazi tyranny, and he was lucky enough to return home.

Preston was an average soldier. He volunteered and became one of about 630,000 Canadians in the Active Army (remember that the Canadian Army was the only volunteer army on the Allied side). He enlisted at 17, and even added one year to his age (most Canadian Army soldiers were between 18 and 25; two-thirds of Canadian Army soldiers had no classes past Grade 7). On a 1993 tour of the Normandy Battlefield, I took particular notice of the gravestones of two Canadian soldiers. One was age 16, and the other was 36. Both of these men were heroes. On account of their ages, they did not have to volunteer to fight a war overseas. But, like Preston, they did.

Preston joined a part of the Canadian Army with "teeth," the Artillery, and not a "tail" support Corps or unit, such as the Engineers, Service Corps, Corps of Signals, Medical Corps, Ordnance, Pay Corps, Postal Corps, Intelligence Corps, and Provost Corps.

Most Canadian Army soldiers served to support infantry regiments, artillery batteries, and tank regiments. (A Canadian Army Infantry Division, comprised of more than 18,000 men, had only 7,400 front-line infantry troops; the rest were support troops.) And the infantry regiments suffered 75 percent of all Canadian Army casualties. So by the summer of 1944, the Canadian Army began its infantry reinforcement crisis.

Preston's Artillery Regiment, the 3rd Light Anti-Aircraft, had, by the end of 1944, become redundant, for the German Air Force possessed a fraction of its once-mighty "Battle of Britain" strength. It had been worn down by aircrew and aircraft attrition on all fronts and unrelenting Allied bombing of German military, industrial, and civilian targets.

Preston, after three years' service in Canada, England, and Europe, was promoted to Sergeant in September 1944. He remained in the Artillery after part of his Regiment was transferred to an infantry reinforcement role to "beef up" Canadian Army infantry regiments savaged by high casualty rates. His Sergeant's rank probably saved him from immediate transfer to an infantry regiment.

Preston was an average soldier. Near the war's end, the infantry reinforcement crisis touched him directly. From January 1945, the 3rd Light Anti-Aircraft Regiment had begun to fire its guns over open sights in a direct fire infantry support role. Just a few days before the end of the war, his "throat dry, with a squeaky voice," Preston himself led a reconnaissance patrol across a field near Oldenburg, Germany. The next day, another patrol leader was shot.

Preston had been wounded by German Army artillery return fire in September 1944. He had lost a close friend, killed by German Air Force bomb fragments, during the Normandy Campaign. Surviving the war was often a matter of chance and circumstance: were you in that long chow line when German fighter-bombers zoomed in on a strafing run, or were you near your Bofors 40 mm cannon and your deeply dug slit trench?

Preston was an average soldier. He endured the privations of army life in Normandy, trying to sleep in deep slit trenches crawling with lice and sand fleas. In better conditions, later in Nijmegen, he would rest easier on straw palliases in civilian barns. His wool battledress uniform jacket and trousers would have been scratchy in summer, not warm enough in winter. Yet Preston enjoyed army life, regarded his time in the army with fondness—for he had survived, and the best was yet to come.

Preston met an English girl in the fall of 1943 and married her in October 1945. He became one of the almost 45,000 Canadians who brought so-called "war brides" back to Canada. In the spring of 1946, Harry and Phyllis began a new life in Toronto, with better luck than the average demobilized Canadian. There was the Army Education Grant, the purchase of a house (all across Canada, an acute housing shortage existed), and better job prospects, which led to a government job in the Post Office. Harry Preston, an average soldier, helped to build the Canada we are now privileged to live in.

Dr. Jack Granatstein, in a Remembrance Day speech given at the Royal Canadian Military Institute, Toronto, November 9, 2011, summed up the extraordinary contribution of the average soldier:

We live in relative peace, in freedom, in prosperity, because Canadians have been willing to fight and die to keep this country secure. This matters every day. We must not forget this.

Gregory Loughton
Curator Emeritus, Royal Canadian Military Institute
Toronto, March 2019

1

Outbreak of the Second World War

On September 1, 1939, Nazi Germany declared war on Poland. Rapidly moving German armored divisions, supported by air power and followed by infantry, struck deep into Polish territory using a new style of warfare called blitzkrieg, or lighting warfare. Britain and France retaliated by declaring war on Germany on September 3. On September 10, Canadian Prime Minister Mackenzie King authorized the declaration of war against Germany, and Canada joined the Allies. The Second World War had begun.

On September 27, the Polish capital of Warsaw surrendered. Polish resistance came to an end by October 6. Germany and the Soviet Union divided Poland between themselves in agreement with the Molotov-Ribbentrop non-aggression pact that had been signed between the two on August 23, 1939. On May 10, 1940, after a lull in fighting, the Germans launched Operation *Fall Gelb* and Operation *Fall Rot*, a two-part offensive across Belgium, Holland, and Luxembourg, flanking the Maginot Line through the Ardennes Forest and into France. The Low Countries capitulated within two weeks. In the process, the Germans encircled and trapped several Allied armies. British commanders, realizing the futility of the situation, recalled the British Expeditionary Force from France. They evacuated from Dunkirk by June 4, alongside other Allied troops. On June 14, 1940, Paris fell to the Germans.

On July 6, 1944, a young Canadian soldier named Harry Preston stepped onto the shores of Normandy as part of the 2nd Canadian Infantry Division. The Allies were driving hard into

Germany's territorial gains thanks to many men like Preston who had never been to Europe—and who would never forget it.

ON A COLD, WET FEBRUARY morning in 2018, I drove to the Sunnybrook Veterans Centre located on Bayview Avenue in Toronto. Opened in 1948 as a war veterans' hospital, Sunnybrook became the largest veterans care facility in Canada. Veterans could apply to live in the centre if their communities could no longer meet their needs. Four-hundred-and-seventy-five veterans from the Second World War and the Korean War lived at the centre at the time of my visit.

Snow blanketed the parkland surrounding the centre. After parking, I walked to the L Wing where I met Kathleen Nimigon, a representative of the centre who had helped me locate a veteran of the Second World War to interview for my research. We walked down a long corridor, empty except for a nurse sitting behind the main desk. We approached a door midway down the hall and Nimigon ushered me in. Beside the door, on a small plaque, was written the name Harry Preston.

I grew up in Karachi, Pakistan. When I was around 12 years old, my parents bought me a colourful book entitled *World War II* by H.P. Willmott, Robin Cross, and Charles Messenger. Over the next few years, I reread it often. I played video games, like *Medal of Honor* and *Call of Duty*, both centred on the Second World War. I obsessed over movies like *Saving Private Ryan* and shows like *Band of Brothers*. I loved reading about the war because it was the last war between good and evil. The Allies encompassed everything good while the Nazis were evil. When I grew up, I realized the war was not so black and white. There were good and bad men and women on both sides, though I understood that Nazism was evil to its core. Throughout high school, I continued studying history, becoming a teacher's assistant for my world history class. While studying at the University of Toronto, I specialized in 20th-century European history and the Second World War. With the help of Nimigon, I could finally talk to a veteran of the war. I entered the room nervous and excited.

The room inside was small but cozy. A television on a dresser blared the CBC news. A bulletin board hung on the wall above a writing table. On the board were pinned pictures of children and families. A black-and-white portrait of a man in military attire hung on the wall between the TV and the writing table, along with a black-and-white photo of a group of around 100 men standing in orderly rows. This was the 15th Light Anti-Aircraft Battery. A small painting of a scene from one of Omar Khayyam's poems stood out amongst the family photos. An iPad mini sat on the coffee table alongside a newspaper crossword puzzle, a potted flower, and two bottles of Red Label. A single window revealed the white landscape outside. Harry Preston, the man I'd come to see, sat on a single-seat couch watching TV.

"Hi Harry, this is *the* student from the University of Toronto. He's come to talk to you about your experiences in the war," Nimigon said.

Preston smiled. "Take a seat and just throw your coat on the bed," he told me.

"Thank you," I replied, pulling up the chair and sitting down.

Preston had a kind face and wore his smart blue shirt tucked into beige khakis. Over that, he wore a black North Face jacket. Even so many decades after the war, his crisp, clean clothes highlighted his military background. His head was covered by a cap and he had a salt and pepper moustache. He sat slumped in his chair, resting his hand on a walker in front of him. I saw the hearing aid in his ear.

"Go ahead and ask me anything," he said.

I conducted three interviews with Preston on February 4, February 24, and April 4, 2018. Each time, Preston welcomed me into the room and let me record our conversations on my phone. During our first meeting, I asked Preston about his childhood. He said it was "average."

HARRY ALFRED PRESTON WAS BORN on April 28, 1922, in Ottawa, Ontario, to Harry Preston Sr. and Hazel Webb. His father fought in the British infantry during the Great War and his mother died five years after he was born while giving birth to his brother. Preston's father remarried and moved to Toronto and then Winnipeg. Preston spent his childhood in Winnipeg where he developed an interest in mathematics, algebra, and geometry. He attended a public school and graduated with his senior matriculation.

Preston told me of his average upbringing in Winnipeg. His father had heart problems and was inconsistent at his job. He received a pension from the army but they were often unable to pay their utility bills and had their water supply cut off. Despite these hardships, Preston said he had a normal childhood. He spent time with his friends, played cards, and went on hikes in the countryside.

AUGUST 1940 – FEBRUARY 1941

In 1940, Preston joined the Winnipeg Militia. Like others in his generation, he had long been interested in joining the military but had been rejected by the air force because he was nearsighted. Preston kept applying.

"Everyone was doing it," Preston said. "All my friends had gone and joined the navy and air force and had been deployed already. It was just the thing to do. They all say it's patriotism, and sure, that was there too, but we did it because it was *the* thing to do. There was a sense of adventure, you know, that you could see the world. And you figure you're doing the right thing."

Above all else, his last sentence resonated with me. The right thing to do. In moments of heightened anxiety, like in war, when emotions and propaganda run wild, how does a person know what is right from what seems right? Doesn't the fog of war play a part in convincing some soldiers to simply do what they're told to do? In retrospect, sailing to Europe to defend Britain from the tyranny of the Nazis was be right thing to do. But the other side thought they were doing the right thing too. I asked Preston how different he felt from the average German soldier. Couldn't they have been friends if circumstances had been different?

"Individually, I couldn't build up any kind of great hate for them," said Preston. "I didn't like their politics and their killing of the Jews and their idea of a master race, but they were the same as us. Everybody's the same."

Since the Winnipeg Militia was unlikely to be deployed to Europe, Preston applied to join the 15th Light Anti-Aircraft Battery, part of the 3rd Light Anti-Aircraft Regiment, which began recruiting in August of 1940.

"By the time I got to the artillery," he chuckled, "I had memorized the eyesight charts."

When the battery accepted him, he was given the rank of Gunner, the equivalent of a Private. At 17, he was too young to join, so on the application forms he added a year to his age. "You had guys as young as 16 in the army, as long as they looked old enough," he said.

Preston's regiment became part of the Sixth Brigade, Second Division, First Canadian Army. In military organizations, army groups are the biggest units. These are followed by armies. Both are commanded by Generals or Field Marshals. The next largest units are divisions, either infantry or armour. In the divisions stand brigades, each with three regiments. Each regiment contains three or four batteries within it. Batteries are then broken down into troops, designated by letters. Altogether, divisions with auxiliary troops usually number around 20,000. In the artillery, the ranks started with the lowest rank of Gunner and rose through Lance Bombardier, Bombardier, Lance Sergeant, and Sergeant.

Preston, a Gunner, received his elementary training for five months in Winnipeg. He studied mathematics, especially trigonometry and geometry, knowledge he'd need to shoot down enemy planes and shell enemy positions. After he completed elementary training, his battery underwent foot and rifle drills.

In December, the battery received Christmas and New Year's leave, but to ensure that they all enjoyed each other's fellowship, commanders held a Christmas dinner on December 21. The soldiers ate turkey and drank beer. After the New Year, they received orders to prepare to ship out. On February 3,

1941, the battery boarded trains and began its journey east to Halifax. At the train station, throngs of thousands bade farewell to their friends and loved ones. Some of the faces beamed while others wept.

The 3rd Light Anti-Aircraft Regiment shipped out of Halifax in late February of 1941. Their destination was England, which was being ravaged by constant bombing. *Their* war was about to begin.

2

Defending Britain

On June 4, 1940, in the aftermath of the "Miracle of Dunkirk" that saw 380,000 Allied soldiers rescued from Nazi capture or death on the beaches of France, British Prime Minister Winston Churchill delivered his carefully crafted and rousing "We Shall Fight on the Beaches" speech to the British House of Commons. He told his fellow citizens:

We shall go on to the end. We shall fight in France, we shall fight on the seas and oceans, we shall fight with growing confidence and growing strength in the air, we shall defend our island, whatever the cost may be. We shall fight on the beaches, we shall fight on the landing grounds, we shall fight in the fields and in the streets, we shall fight in the hills; we shall never surrender.

Contrary to popular belief, his speech was not broadcast live over the radio. The recording available today was not recorded until 1949. Instead, a report of the speech was broadcast to the British public, and it left them in a sombre and pessimistic mood. It also had mixed responses in the House of Commons. However, it was arguably not geared for either. The historian Richard Toye argues that Churchill wrote the speech to inspire the Americans to join the war by highlighting his country's resolve. The speech was well received in the U.S. The press went into raptures and the public praised and discussed it at length. President Franklin Delano Roosevelt liked it too.

With the evacuation of Dunkirk, and the fall of continental Europe, the Germans were now positioned on the English

Channel. In August 1940, Adolf Hitler began making plans to invade England by sea. To win Britain, Hitler ordered the head of the Luftwaffe, Hermann Göring, to attain air superiority over British skies. Thus began the Blitz, or the Battle of Britain. The German Air Force bombed and destroyed port facilities, industrial centres, and airfields. Terry Copp, a history professor at Wilfrid Laurier University, called the Blitz "the first systematic bombing campaign against a civilian population in history."

The German Luftwaffe used its medium bombers—the Heinkel He 111, the Dornier Do 17, the Junkers Ju 88—to devastate the United Kingdom. The Messerschmitt Bf 109s, its staple single-engine fighters, matched the British Spitfires in terms of speed and handling. However, the Messerschmitt's abilities were hampered by its limited range. German bombers also proved too vulnerable without fighter escorts. The Junker Ju 87, the Luftwaffe's dive bomber, proved too slow for air combat and was withdrawn.

While the Germans commanded a numerical advantage over the Royal Air Force, the British leveraged their numbers effectively. The Luftwaffe deployed 2,422 aircraft against the RAF, which could field 226 Spitfires and 353 Hurricanes. British Spitfires and Hurricanes were exceptionally equipped with 1,030 hp Rolls-Royce Merlin III engines, could fly at speeds of 575 kph and 529 kph respectively, and carried Browning .303 machine guns. They were maneuverable, capable of absorbing damage, and had all-round visibility. In combat, the Spitfire matched the Messerschmitt Bf 109's capabilities, though the Hurricane was slower. Unlike the Germans, the British had the home-ground advantage and were able to refuel, rearm, and resupply their aircraft more often, which made the difference in battle. On August 20, 1940, in a speech to the House of Commons, Churchill paid homage to the RAF with words that became famous: "Never in the field of human conflict was so much owed by so many to so few."

By September 1940, in the face of a stoic defence mounted by the Royal Air Force, Hitler realized that he could not bomb Britain into surrendering and indefinitely postponed the invasion of England. But that did not put an end to the bombing. From September 1940 to May 1941, the Luftwaffe continued bombing cities across England, but not for the purpose of invading. Instead, they wanted to subdue Britain's morale and its ability to wage war. Entire cities lay in ruin. On May 10, 1941, 1,436 civilians died in a single bombing raid on the capital. By June of 1941, Hitler had plans for invading the Soviet Union. Most of the Luftwaffe transferred east in preparation for the attack, granting England some reprieve. Germany was ascendant.

1 MARCH 1941 – FALL 1943

Preston's battery arrived in England on March 1, 1941, near the end of Germany's air attack. The battery was transported to Colchester, 144 kilometres north of London where the troops began their intensive training on their main weapon: the Bofors 40 mm anti-craft multipurpose cannon. The basic model was on a fixed-ground mount, from which an inner platform rotated the gun 360 degrees. These were towed by a 4x4 truck. Later models could be mounted on the Crusader tank. With a two-rounds-per-second firing capacity, as few as two soldiers could man the gun, although ideally a seven-man team operated it. The set up took two minutes for direct fire over open sights and 30 minutes for full indirect fire.

Preston's regiment received predictor and deployment training as well. Predictor training taught soldiers how to shoot planes out of the air. "You see, you don't shoot at the enemy plane, you shoot where they're going to be when your shell gets there," Preston said. "That's the whole secret of anti-aircraft."

The devastation of the Blitz of London shocked Preston. Buildings left standing were surrounded by rubble. Londoners lived through a surreal moment. "You'd go down into the subway, or the tube as they called it," Preston said, "and the people were sleeping in the stations. They'd leave enough room to walk by the tracks though."

Preston was issued with a bolt action Lee-Enfield Mk.I rifle, a Sten Mk.II submachine gun, and a box of hand grenades. For the first six months, his regiment was attached to the British anti-aircraft divisions and the troops used their Bofors until his division received their own. After their training and drills, the regiment supported defensive positions in various towns along the Channel Coast.

"The Messerschmitt 109s came low over the waves, because they wanted to avoid being seen by the radars," he informed me about the coastal raids. "Usually they came in ones and twos and they'd drop a bomb quickly and scoot off. It was just a nuisance, to let people know that they could still do something."

During his time in England, Preston became accustomed to sleeping on canvas bags stuffed with straw called palliasses. The army provided a wool blanket to go along with them. Some officers slept in sleeping bags. A typical day's diet consisted of porridge for breakfast, and mutton, potatoes, and bread for lunch and dinner. Beer was also widely available. While stationed along the coast, Preston spent time fishing too.

"Sometimes we used to get this big Polish sausage. We used to call it horse cock," he said, laughing.

Nineteen-forty-one was a significant year for the Allies. On June 22, Germany broke its non-aggression pact and launched an ill-fated invasion of the Soviet Union under the codename Operation Barbarossa. Field Marshal Ritter von Leeb's Army Group North had as its objective the capture of Leningrad (today named Saint Petersburg) in the Soviet northwest. Field Marshal Fedor von Bock's Army Group Center was tasked with crushing the Red Army in Belarus and taking Smolensk. Field Marshal Gerd von Rundstedt's Army Group South's aim was to invade Ukraine, capture Kiev, and seize the oil-rich industrial regions of the Volga, Donetz, and Caucasus.

And then on December 7, 1941, Japan launched a surprise attack on the U.S. naval base at Pearl Harbor in Honolulu, Hawaii. U.S. President Roosevelt, along with Congress, declared war on Japan the next day. Germany, in keeping with the Tripartite Pact, declared war on the U.S. on December 11. The course of the war changed entirely.

On August 19, 1942, Canadian and British forces numbering around 6,000 attempted to gather intelligence and raise morale by raiding the French port city of Dieppe. The Second Canadian Infantry Division was part of the attack on Dieppe, but Preston was on leave. Allied commanders initially postponed the attack twice and were afraid it would raise suspicion if they postponed the attack a third time, and so they didn't cancel any leaves when the raid actually commenced. Preston was away seeing his great-uncle in Britain. Preston said he knew that something was happening because he saw soldiers and ships amassing along the coastal train route he was travelling.

"Did you feel lucky that you didn't go to Dieppe, knowing now what happened?" I asked.

"No, no, I felt left out. All my friends had gone," he answered.

The answer surprised me. The Dieppe Raid ended disastrously, with the Canadians suffering 3,369 casualties from the approximately 5,000 men who had embarked on the raid. But, as J.L. Granatstein, a professor of history at York University, and Desmond Morton, former principal of Erindale College (now the University of Toronto Mississauga), surmised, the Dieppe Raid was a costly lesson for the Allies, yet it was one that was needed to learn of the importance of detailed planning and execution—one that would pay dividends on the beaches of Normandy two years later.

Until the invasion of Normandy on June 6, 1944, Preston's regiment continued defending various British coastal towns and cities from Luftwaffe raids. Preston spent his free time in England going to the cinema and drinking at pubs. Twice in five years, he went to an army show where there was either a dancer, singer, or comedian. These army shows, sanctioned by the Department of National Defence in 1942, aimed at entertaining and motivating Canadian soldiers. The military created "The Canadian Army Radio Show," a variety radio show that broadcast weekly from Montreal on the CBC. Success on the radio led to the creation of a touring version that brought entertainment and morale to men fighting on the front lines in Northwest Europe for the remainder of the war.

Preston made a dollar and a quarter per day in the army and 35 or so dollars a month. He signed half of his pay over to his father and kept 15 or so dollars a month for himself. A promotion up the ranks bought soldiers a few extra cents with each rank. Preston spent most of his money on beer. At the time, a pint cost 9 pence.

In the fall of 1943, Preston took two weeks' leave and went to Leeds with his friend Johnny Clemen.

"We went to a pub for a beer. There was a group of three or four girls on the next table and they started talking to us. One of the girls asked, 'How would you like to come home and meet my folks?' and I thought, who's going to refuse her?"

Her name was Phyllis Turgoose. Preston spent a week of his leave with her.

BY 1943, THE SOVIETS ABSORBED the German thrust and began to effectively counterattack. Stalingrad (now Volgograd), on the Volga River, became a site of a bitter struggle. By the end of January 1943, the Soviets trapped the German 6th Army in Stalingrad and forced its surrender. The Battle of Kursk, the largest tank battle in history, ended with a Soviet victory in July of 1943. From then on, the Soviets went on the offensive, slowly pushing the Germans out of their country. By January 1944, the Siege of Leningrad lifted. Elsewhere, after wiping out Nazi encampments in North Africa, Allied troops landed in Sicily in September 1943, and began advancing north.

"What did you think about the Soviets?" I asked Preston.

"I admired them," he replied. "When their war started, I thought they'd last a couple of weeks, but 80 percent of the German casualties were on the Eastern Front. I am eternally grateful to them. I'd still be fighting there if it wasn't for them."

3

Landings at Normandy

1 JUNE 1944 – 6 JUNE 1944

In preparation for the Normandy Landings, on June 6, 1944, Supreme Commander of the Allied Forces, Dwight D. Eisenhower, in a speech to his men, said:

Soldiers, Sailors, and Airmen of the Allied Expeditionary Force: You are about to embark upon the Great Crusade, toward which we have striven these many months. The eyes of the world are upon you. The hopes and prayers of liberty-loving people everywhere march with you [...] But this is the year 1944. Much has happened since the Nazi triumphs of 1940-41. The United Nations have inflicted upon the Germans great defeats, in open battle [...] The tide has turned. The free men of the world are marching together to victory.

Eisenhower was right. The tide had turned. The Allies made serious gains all across Europe. Normandy would define how quickly the war would end.

On June 6, known as D-Day, the Western Allies, including the U.S., Britain, and Canada, launched Operation Overlord, the largest amphibious invasion in history, in an effort to open up a second front. The Americans landed on Utah Beach and Omaha Beach, where they faced fierce resistance. The British attacked Sword Beach and Gold Beach. The Canadians, spearheaded by the Canadian 3rd Division, attacked Juno Beach. In total, 150,000 Allied troops participated in the invasion.

Preston did not take part in the D-Day landings. His division, weakened after the Dieppe Raid, was left out of the initial assault. "They had us stationed around Dover to fool the Germans that we were going to go across on the narrow part of the Channel and attack Pas-de-Calais. We left our guns all out in the open so they could see," Preston said.

The Germans were aware that an attack launched from Britain was being planned. They just did not know when or where it would come. Preston's regiment was part of a larger Allied plan codenamed Fortitude. Fortitude intended to divert attention away from Normandy and convince the Germans that the attack would come at Calais. Fake radio signals emitted from Dover suggested a large military buildup. U.S. General George Patton was given command of an entire fictitious Army Group stationed around Dover. The pinnacle of the deception was the hundreds of realistic dummy tanks and equipment that the Allies left in open fields for German reconnaissance to photograph. The plan worked. Even after the landings at Normandy, Hitler refused to order divisions to reinforce Normandy, believing that Normandy was a ploy and the real attack was coming at Calais.

In the preparation for D-Day, a bizarre and seemingly inexplicable incident occurred. *The Daily Telegraph*, a British newspaper, published a crossword puzzle in May. One of the clues asked for the name of a U.S. state. The answer was Utah. Later that month, another clue asked for the name of a Native American tribe on the Missouri. The answer was Omaha. Further clues were answered with "Overlord," "Mulberry," and "Neptune," all codewords for various parts of the invasion plan.

This set alarm bells ringing in the Allied high command because the entire plan hinged on the idea of deception and secrecy. Britain's Security Service, the MI5, began an inquiry and interrogated the two school masters who compiled the crossword puzzles. They were eventually cleared. Their choice of clues was just an incredible coincidence. Even then, doubts lingered amongst sections of the British intelligence.

2 JULY 1944 – 15 JULY 1944

Preston's regiment set sail from Tilbury on July 2, 1944. A stream of ships led the way to the coast of France. By this time, Preston was a Sergeant, one of the highest ranks amongst the non-commissioned officers, a rank he maintained for the rest of the war. By July, the Allied armies had cleared the beaches and moved inland, so Preston's landing was unobstructed. His landing ship became separated from the others and Preston had to ask civilians if they had seen guns similar to his. After a few hours, he was able to find his regiment and set up the Bofors.

"Did you feel special coming ashore at Normandy?" I asked.

"It's what we'd been waiting for. You didn't feel like you were doing much sitting in Britain, although we were on our guns all the time. We did a lot more than the infantry then. They just sat there waiting. But we were all eager to do something."

On the night of July 10, the Second Division advanced and positioned itself along the Caen-Bayeux road with its centre at the Carpiquet Airdrome. They were positioned behind a ridge overlooking the Orne River and the airfields. Their positioning was ideal as it allowed for effective camouflaging and conceal-ment. The same night, 11 German Messerschmitts descended on them in ones and twos. They had most likely been on a recon-naissance mission and were flying low. All the guns in the regi-ment opened fire at almost point-blank range. It was Preston's first action on the continent.

"We brought down four or five of them, though the regi-mental history says we knocked down seven, but that's pretty high for my thinking."

On the front lines, Preston was issued with a "compo pack," or a composition pack. It contained a few tins of meat and veg-etables, corned beef, hard biscuits, chocolate, pudding, and a pack of 50 cigarettes. Without a kitchen, the soldiers relied on their composition packs to keep up their strength during the fighting. They were also issued with a kit bag that included spare clothes, blankets, and a small sewing kit to patch up their uniforms. Unlike the infantry, who carried their equipment on them, Preston's regiment left their backpacks, heavy equipment, supplies, and ammunition on the trucks that pulled their guns. On the front, they dug trenches and fox holes and placed makeshift doors on top to protect themselves from mortar fire.

"My friend Tex McKenzie was killed in Normandy because he couldn't get into the hole fast enough when the bombs started falling," Preston told me.

"Did that affect you?" I asked.

"No, I expected it."

On July 12, six more Messerschmitts appeared and Preston's regiment shot down three. On July 14, a group of Messerschmitts and Focke-Wulfs made a run. Preston's regiment shot down eight. This time the Germans inflicted casualties on the Canadian infantry with their machine guns.

Preston's regiment received new orders. They organized themselves and headed south towards Caen.

4

Breaking Out of Normandy

The city of Caen in Northwest France was one of the main objectives for the Allies on D-Day. Situated just beyond the beaches of Normandy, the city offered a strategic centre for taking the battle inland. Fanatical German resistance delayed any breakthrough, and it took all of June for the Allies to advance inland from the beaches.

Nine days earlier, in preparation for a general advance, the Allied Air Force launched a massive bombing campaign on the city of Caen. "It was a big night raid. I saw many of our Lancasters getting shot down. By the time we went through there, it was just rubble. I imagine the infantry faced some opposition, but when we went through it was clear. We moved pretty fast because we had to get to the other side to get after Falaise," Preston said.

During the Battle for Caen, Preston assisted the infantry and the armour. (Armour referred to tanks—the Canadian Army's main battle tank was the Sherman—armoured personnel carriers, half-tracks, and other mechanized units.) With the Luftwaffe severely weakened, Preston's regiment shifted focus towards ground operations and also operated as an artillery unit.

"We shelled the enemy lines. We'd send an observer towards the front and we'd fire and he'd tell us where our shells were landing so we could correct our aim. That was called indirect shooting. Half the time though, we shot over open sights, without an observer. Then we'd scoot off before the Germans could line up on us."

On July 20, the Canadians finally captured Caen. On July 25, General Patton's 3rd Army broke out of St. Lo and advanced into Brittany. This movement threatened the German left flank. Commander of the German Army in the West, Field Marshal Günther von Kluge, begged Hitler to allow him to retreat from Normandy and form a defensive line past the Seine River. Hitler refused and ordered him to mount a counteroffensive. Kluge's hasty offensive at Mortain caught the Americans off guard and the Germans advanced for 10 kilometres, forming a bulge in the Allied lines. But the German offensive inadvertently gave the Allies the advantage. As the next day dawned, scores of Allied aircraft took to the skies and halted the German attack, leaving four panzer divisions at the mercy of the Americans who now surrounded them.

British General Bernard Montgomery, commander of the Allied ground operations, realized that the Germans could be trapped. His plan called for the Canadians to seize Falaise and unite with the Americans at Argentan. The British would prevent the Germans from striking further west. This would trap the Germans in a pocket. (A pocket, in military terms, refers to an army that has been cut off from its base and other Allied forces by an opposing army. These armies were usually flanked by the opposing army and then encircled and trapped. They were known as pockets because when studying a map, it became clear that the positions of the surrounded forces resembled a pocket. A pocket was also known as a "gap" or "cauldron.")

In the Second World War, with the advent of blitzkrieg or lightning warfare, pockets became more widespread. With fast-moving, mobile troops, the Germans often flanked and over-ran entire armies by punching straight through their front lines. After encircling them, they would continue to attack them from all sides until the besieged army surrendered. This method was effective in forcing the surrender of thousands of troops.

On August 7, the Canadian attack on Falaise began at night. "When the attack started, our job was to fire five or six rounds every five minutes for the armour to follow the tracer," Preston said. Tracers were an illuminating projectile, easily visible to the naked eye at night and in the day and used to guide armour and infantry towards an intended target. The 2nd Canadian Division attacked with six long columns of Sherman tanks and "Kangaroo" armoured personnel carriers (APC), all supported by an artillery barrage. The 12th SS Panzer Division had dug into the Verrières Ridge, an advantageous position between the Canadians and Falaise. From this position, they blunted the Canadian attack.

On August 8, American Boeing B-17 Flying Fortress bombers, attempting to aid the Allied advance, released their payload early due to a navigation mistake. "I climbed up into a tower," Preston said, "to get a closer look at what was happening. I saw them dropping their bombs behind us and then continue towards us. Our regiment lost 12 men, and it slowed the attack for four hours."

I asked Preston if death by friendly fire was common. "Yes," he told me, "especially when the Americans did it. Unlike the British, the American bombers came in huge numbers and they dropped their bombs all together. They used to drop anti-personnel bombs, which were the size of a nickel but twice as thick. They did a lot of damage."

On August 16, Kluge was finally allowed to retreat. It was too late. Derek Blizard, a veteran of the British Army and a writer, wrote about the incident: "The next three days saw the most terrible destruction of the German armies."

On August 17, the Canadian forces finally broke through and captured Falaise. They captured Chambois the next day. In the south, the Americans seized Argentan and, on August 19, they united with the Canadians. The entire German 7th Army and the 5th Panzer Army were surrounded in the Falaise Pocket. Despite a momentary breakthrough by the Germans, the Allies sealed off the pocket completely by August 20. The Allied Air Force and artillery pummelled the trapped Germans for the next three days, turning the main road from Mortain, all the way to Chambois, into a nightmarish killing ground of torn limbs, rivers of blood, and mountains of rotting flesh.

At the end of the Battle of the Falaise Pocket, 10,000 Germans lay dead with another 50,000 taken prisoner. Eight infantry divisions and two panzer divisions were captured almost in their entirety.

C.P. Stacey, the author of the official history of the Canadian Army in the Second World War, writes: "The whole vicinity of St. Lambert (an area held by elements of the Canadian army) was covered with the human and material debris of an army which had suffered the greatest disaster in modern military history."

After the fighting ended, Preston marched the road from Falaise. Bombed out German Tiger tanks and half-tracks, the remains of the once-feared panzer divisions, broken-down trucks, dead horses, and the bodies of dead German soldiers, cluttered the road. "I remember the smell the most," Preston said. "All the bodies were rotting, and it was an awful stink."

Eisenhower, who visited the pocket after the fighting ended, was sickened by the carnage and described the scene as something out of Dante's *Inferno*. "It was literally possible to walk for hundreds of yards at a time, stepping on nothing but dead and decaying flesh," he remarked in his memoirs.

The Battle for Normandy was over. Since D-Day, 250,000 German troops were killed or wounded and another 200,000 captured. Altogether, the best part of 40 divisions were destroyed. Allied losses in Normandy totalled approximately 209,000. The Canadians lost nearly 16,000 men.

By the time the Normandy campaign finished, the Luftwaffe had been handicapped. Since the assault on Juno Beach, the Canadian infantry had been on the front lines and their numbers had thinned. They needed reinforcements. The Canadian government, afraid of dissent in Quebec, chose not to conscript young men into the military. This had been a problem Prime Minister Robert Borden had faced as he tried to recruit troops for the Armed Forces in the First World War: the Quebecois felt it was not their responsibility to fight for the British. The 1941 Canadian federal election was the first and only time Preston voted Conservative. Unlike King's Liberals, the Conservatives promised to begin conscription and send reinforcements, and

Preston knew the military needed conscription if they were to win the war. Granatstein and Morton detail excerpts from soldiers who expressed severe discontentment at the lack of reinforcements and blamed King and the Liberals. In the meantime, the Canadian Army began to transfer men from the anti-air regiments to the infantry. It was not until November 1944 that King finally bent to the demand and enacted conscription amidst much opposition.

"They cut our strength in half and most of our guys went to the infantry or other regiments. The officers called us out in the field and read out the names of the guys who had to go, with tears running down their faces, because they were breaking up the regiment. But I stayed with the anti-air."

5

Advance to Germany

By closing the Falaise Pocket, the Allies broke the bottleneck at Normandy. The U.S. 3rd Army advanced to Paris and liberated it on August 25. The British advanced into Belgium, liberating Brussels on September 3. The Canadian forces, including the 2nd Division, advanced east to cross the Seine River at Rouen. On August 26, the Canadian 2nd Division met stiff resistance from the 331st German Infantry Division, which held the high ground at Forêt de la Londe, just south of Rouen.

On August 29, the Germans made a tactical withdrawal from Rouen. Preston was stationed with his gun on a small bridge at Forêt de la Londe when his position was attacked by the Luftwaffe, in an attempt to hamper the Allied supply lines and their advance.

"Eight to 12 planes appeared in ones and twos and dropped flares. You think you're the only person in the world when you're standing under the flares. But they're above and you can't see them. There was also a German or French sympathizer in the bushes nearby and he kept pointing a flashlight towards us. I think he was trying to direct their fire," Preston said.

"What did you do?" I asked.

"I was about to take a shot at him with my rifle, but then I didn't."

"Why not?"

"I don't know. I think it was too late at that point. The planes were already there and it wouldn't have made a difference."

"Do you think you could have shot him?"

"Oh, yeah, I think I could have. Maybe I was too busy on the Bofors."

"Did you ever shoot anyone with your rifle or sidearm during the war?"

"Never."

"Do you think it was easier to shoot someone using the Bofors, rather than your rifle?"

"No, I could have shot somebody with my rifle. You have to or they kill you, you know?"

The regiment shot down none of the planes, and none of Preston's comrades were injured.

Two days later, on August 31, the Allies took Rouen and thousands of cheering French civilians celebrated their liberation. Two months after arriving in Normandy, Preston got the chance to shower for the first time.

"They'd set up a pump by a river from where they attached pipes and we'd shower there. There'd be a table with uniforms, underwear, and socks and we'd pick them up after showering," he told me.

The First Canadian Army moved through Rouen quickly.

One of the strangest things Preston saw while in France was seeing a plane fall out of the sky. "I was sitting on the gun one sunny day, somewhere in the north of France. I couldn't hear any shooting or anything. Out of the sky comes a Messerschmitt at a 90-degree angle. He flew straight into the ground. He didn't shoot or do anything. I don't know where he came from. He wasn't in any dog fight. It's one thing that struck me."

1 SEPTEMBER 1944 – 2 NOVEMBER 1944

By the first week of September, the Allies advanced too quickly and overstretched their supply lines. Supplies still came from the town of Cherbourg in Normandy. The Canadians were tasked with capturing the French and Belgian channel ports to alleviate the supply issue. They were unable to capture the ports quickly, though, as Hitler had declared them *Festungen* or fortresses and ordered that they be held to the last man. Even when they were captured, the port facilities were useless because the Germans had destroyed them.

General Montgomery decided that the Dutch port of Antwerp would be the solution to their supply problems. On September 4, British troops occupied Antwerp. But Antwerp was an inland port, situated 32 kilometers from the estuary where the Scheldt River met the North Sea. The Allies seized the port, but the Germans dug in on both sides of the Scheldt—any ship entering the river would be subjected to artillery fire from both sides for 32 kilometers before reaching Antwerp. On September 16, Montgomery tasked the Canadians with clearing both sides of the Scheldt.

"The fighting was quite heavy there. They wanted to keep us from using the port as long as they could," Preston told me.

While fighting at Bergen op Zoom, an area near Antwerp, Preston used the method of indirect firing. As he worked his gun, an enemy shell hit a house next to his position, showering him in shrapnel.

"I think I was knocked out. I remember laying down, waking up and looking up at the guy looking down at me wondering how bad it was."

He never reported the injury, claiming it was not significant. It was the first and last time Preston was injured during the war.

On November 2, the 2nd Division was relieved and sent to Perk in Belgium. The Germans were cleared from the Scheldt and the first Allied supply ships arrived on November 26.

9 NOVEMBER 1944 – JANUARY 1945

After resting at Perk, the 2nd Division received new orders: to take a holding position in Nijmegen, a city not far from the German border. On November 9, the division arrived in Nijmegen and relieved the British troops there. They dug their guns in, fortified their positions, and made preparations for winter. The front lines remained static for the winter and neither side made any significant advances in the area. Preston set up his gun near a barn, where he had a good field of fire, and then holed up for the winter.

"The farmer, whose barn it was, called us into his house to sleep there. We'd eat with him and his family, and we spent the worst part of the winter there, while most of the guys were out in the trenches. We still had to man the gun of course, and sometimes we'd fire off some rounds at the front, which we called harassing fire. But that winter was pretty comfortable," he said.

In the south, on December 16, the Germans launched the last gasp Ardennes Offensive, catching the Americans completely off guard. The Ardennes Offensive, or the Battle of the Bulge, was Germany's last major offensive in the war. Commanded by Field Marshal Gerd von Rundstedt, Sepp Dietrich's 6th SS Panzer Army, and Erich von Manteuffel's 5th SS Panzer Army struck deep into the Ardennes Forest with the ultimate aim of capturing Liège and Antwerp and splitting the Americans and British. Eisenhower believed it was a repeat of the audacious 1940 blitzkrieg of France and the Low Countries, an attack that stunned the Allies and subdued Western Europe. Both the 1940 attack and the 1944 attack were led by Rundstedt. The Allied Air Force, unable to fly in the stormy weather, languished on the ground. The Germans made a large salient in the American lines and surrounded Bastogne, an important centre of communications. Despite the intense pressure, the defenders at Bastogne held out, and once the weather cleared, the Allied Air Force attacked and bombed the Germans. On December 26, General George Patton's army relieved the American forces at Bastogne and broke the German momentum. By the start of January, the Germans were repulsed. They could never again mount an offensive.

8 FEBRUARY 1945 – 8 MAY 1945

In January 1945, the Canadian forces prepared for a spring offensive into Germany. Operation Veritable launched on February 8, with the aim of clearing the area between Nijmegen and the Lower Rhine. Running ahead of the infantry's advance, the 3rd

Light Anti-Aircraft Regiment took part in a massive 1,000-gun artillery barrage. The infantry attacked and seized the town of Kleve before running into opposition in the Reichswald, a wooded area where the German 84th Infantry Division constructed five lines of defence, dug trenches and anti-tank ditches, and fortified positions.

A month later, on March 4, the Allies finally cleared the Reichswald, and Preston's regiment received two weeks' rest. On March 23, the regiment began to cross the Rhine. Once across, they marched steadily north to Groningen, facing minimal resistance. From April 23 until the end of the war in Europe, the 3rd Light Anti-Aircraft Regiment functioned as an infantry brigade. They were left with the task of clearing the German North Sea coast.

On April 30, with Soviet shells raining down on Berlin, Hitler committed suicide by biting on a cyanide capsule and then shooting himself in the head.

In the first week of May, Preston was placed in charge of a patrol, south of the German town of Oldenburg. While on patrol, they encountered German soldiers who hadn't yet surrendered.

"The most I was scared was when I had to take a patrol across a field. My voice got all squeaky and my throat got all dry. The Germans were in a house on the other side of the field from where they'd been shooting at us. They took off when they saw us coming. It was just before the end of the war, so I figure they didn't want to be the last ones killed on the Western Front. So, we didn't shoot at them either. We checked the house, and it was clear. When I got back and reported to my commander, he was happy and gave me half a bottle of gin," he said, laughing.

After taking the patrol and drinking the gin, Preston slept soundly. When he awoke the next morning, he found out that another patrol was sent. The officer who took that patrol got shot through the face.

Preston could have been the one who died, and if he had, that would have been the way it went. "You just take what comes," Preston said. "They used to say in the first war, 'If a shell's got your number on it, you're going to get it.' You're going to die at some point. You just do your duty."

On May 3, the regiment received word that the Germans had evacuated the area. Preston's regiment was ordered to hold their positions. General Harry Crerar, commander of the First Canadian Army, declared in a message to his troops on May 4 that the war was nearly over:

From the beaches of Dieppe to those of Normandy and from thence through Northern France, Belgium, Holland and north-west Germany [...] crushing and complete victory over the German enemy has been secured. In rejoicing at this supreme accomplishment, we shall remember the friends who have paid the full price for the belief they also held that no sacrifice in the interest of the principles of which we fought could be too great.

On May 6, the 3rd Light Anti-Aircraft Regiment stood down after 11 months on the continent. The regiment's official history concludes with the statement: "May the regiment, mighty in conflict, prove itself as noble in peace!"

On May 8, Nazi Germany surrendered unconditionally to the Allies, ending the Second World War in Europe. From June 1944 to May 1945, the First Canadian Army marched across Europe, from the shores of Normandy, through France, Belgium, Holland, and finally past the Rhine and into Germany. By the end of the war, the army numbered 170,000 men. Stacey surmises that from D-Day until Victory in Europe Day, the Canadian Army in the Northwest Europe Campaign suffered 48,000 casualties of which around 12,000 were fatal. Out of Eisenhower's 90 divisions, the Canadians only fielded five. Despite the smaller contribution of soldiers by a small country, the Canadians faced some of the fiercest fighting and helped to liberate Western Europe from Nazi tyranny.

"Many a home across Canada had been darkened by these tragic losses; but the bereaved were not without consolation," Stacey concludes in his history of the war. "A tyranny, callous and cruel almost beyond belief, which had menaced the whole free world, had been brought down in ruin; and the way lay open—if men were wise enough to see it—to 'broader lands and better days.'"

THE HOLOCAUST

One of the great evils of the Second World War was the Holocaust, the systematic destruction of the Jewish people at the hands of the Nazis. Concentration and extermination camps were set up across Germany, Poland, and other Nazi-held regions. Prisoners included Jews, gypsies, homosexuals, Slavs, prisoners of war, political opponents, the disabled, and any non-Aryans who the Nazis deemed subhuman. The weak, old, and sick were killed immediately in massive gas chambers while the rest worked in forced labour camps for the Nazi industrial machine.

The Allies learned of the existence of the camps from escaped prisoners and refugees. When news of Auschwitz spread, the Allies considered bombing the railways and the gas chambers, but no such action occurred, mostly because the air force doubted its ability to accurately bomb the intended targets.

Professor Rebecca Wittmann, chair of the history department at the University of Toronto Mississauga and a specialist in the history of the Holocaust, described the Allied response to the concentration camps as a humanitarian action that garnered little support by the men waging war against the Nazis. "[The Allied commanders] certainly knew [about the genocide], and they discussed bombing Auschwitz and its railways, but they used flimsy excuses, stating that the most important thing was to defeat the Germans, and that would end the horrors. I think they could have accurately bombed the railways. My feeling is, that there was no comprehension of the scope and of the racial aspect of the program. I think it has much more to do with it not being a priority. It is rarely a priority to make purely humanitarian efforts at the expense of military moves. The priority was to defeat the Germans."

Terry Copp reports that outside of the small circle of politicians and diplomats, little of what was happening to the Jews of Europe was known to the world. Eventually in August 1942, *The Montreal Star* ran a story with the headline "Nazi Slaughterhouse—Germans Massacre Million Jews in Extermination Drive." However, Copp states, "Hearing or reading about such atrocities did not necessarily mean believing in them." One of the great regrets of the war involves the Holocaust. Could the Allies have done more, sooner, to prevent, or slow, the genocide?

With the Soviets in the east and the Allies in the west, steadily pushing further into previously Nazi-controlled regions, it was only a matter of time until the world truly learned of the brutal realities of the Holocaust. The Red Army was the first to discover one of the camps at Majdanek in Poland, in the summer of 1944. They also liberated Auschwitz, the largest of the camps, in January 1945. It was not until April 15, 1945, when the British forces liberated Bergen-Belsen, that the world truly discovered the horrors of the Final Solution. Canadian troops arrived days later and aided the British in assisting the survivors. Many Canadians wrote stark testimonies of the horrors they witnessed at Bergen-Belsen. Hitler's Final Solution caused the death of approximately 5.7 million Jews and at least another million from various groups.

"By this point, the Germans had surrendered and so the Allies took over the camps and turned them into displaced persons camps," Wittmann said. "They turned Dachau into a prisoner camp for captured SS officers. They had several trials at Dachau where they tried them for their crimes."

In my third interview, I asked Preston about the Holocaust. He said that when he learned the full scale, he was disgusted by what the Nazis did, but like other soldiers, he was largely uninformed about the truth of the matter while the fighting was still ongoing.

"We only found out about the camps when the Russians captured one and then the Americans captured another. But it was kept pretty secret at first. I can't remember where, but we went to a small camp once where the inmates had shot the commander and his girlfriend. We were supposed to do something, but we just congratulated them."

"Let everyone, inside and outside Germany, look upon the work of the Beast," read an editorial in *The Halifax Herald*. "Let there be no more talk about 'just propaganda' and 'these things can't be true.' It is not 'propaganda' and these things are true, overwhelming in their proportions, ghastly in conception, execution and results."

6

Homecoming

Demobilization began soon after May 8, a day known as "Victory in Europe Day." Preston returned to England where he took a job as a transient kitchen caretaker in a barrack at Aldershot. Troops returning from the continent would stop there while waiting to ship back to Canada. The troops who volunteered to ship off to the Pacific theatre of war against the Japanese were prioritized.

On October 6, 1945, Preston married Phyllis Turgoose, the girl he met in a pub in Leeds in 1943, in a small wedding at an Anglican church, in England. They had a party afterwards at his wife's house.

"When did you decide you wanted to marry her?" I asked.

"I think she decided. I never proposed. She's the one who said, 'I think we should get married' and I just said yes. She got me at a weak moment."

"How was the honeymoon?"

"I won't tell you," he replied, laughing.

Preston arrived in Toronto, where he was discharged from the army, in the spring of 1946. His wife followed him to Canada and they bought a house in the city for $5,300. He joined Dominion Wheel and Foundry, where he moulded steel. Within his first year there, he started coughing up lead dust and decided to leave the foundry.

Preston then joined Acme Screw and Gear and made gears for car transmissions. The company also made parts for Massey Harris, a tractor manufacturer. Two years later, Preston took courses in business, arithmetic, and bookkeeping for free because he was a veteran. He was promoted to an inspector in the same factory as a result of his education.

To close my third and final interview with Preston, I asked him how he adjusted back to civilian life.

"It was a little difficult adjusting back. You miss the army. You miss all the people you spent all those days with. I think of the war and the death, but it doesn't bother me. I liked it. It was a good life," he replied.

In 1953, Preston joined the Post Office. He wrote the carrier and clerks exams.

"They asked me if I wanted to be a clerk or a carrier. Clerks made a little more money but they were always inside, and I liked working outside so I took the carriers job. The height of my career was as a letter carrier. I loved the job."

He worked as a letter carrier for 33 years. He sold his house in 1991 and moved into an apartment near St. Lawrence Market. In 1997, his wife passed away at the age of 75.

"We went downtown for supper one Saturday night, and the next morning at 6:00, she grabbed her chest and said, 'My heart, my heart,' and flopped back. She was dead by noon."

In 2015, Preston suffered a stroke. Rendered unable to care for himself, he applied to live at Sunnybrook Veterans Centre.

"I got into Sunnybrook a week after I applied. I was really cuckoo when I came here because of the stroke. It really affected my body and especially my brain. The doctors found brain damage. I was having terrible nightmares. But all that's cleared up pretty well now," he said.

"Do you like it here?" I asked.

"The last year has been good. I've been healthy and I've taken part in all the therapy. They have glass working classes, art classes, and woodworking classes here. They're good because they keep your hands and mind busy."

Preston and Phyllis had three children, two girls and one boy. One of his daughters died. His other children visit often.

"My daughter's the best. Girls are the best. She's always here looking after me. My son was in the real estate business. He went to Mexico for a few years and then he went to Africa for 13 years where he worked in a gold mine. He's down in Costa Rica right now, but when he's in Toronto, he visits every week-end and we play cards and get a beer together," he said, with a smile.

Preston resides on the second floor of the Sunnybrook Veterans Centre where he spends his time playing chess on his iPad, doing crossword puzzles in the newspaper, and watching the news on his television. He likes walking around the building and enjoys getting coffee from the Tim Hortons located in the cafeteria.

The last time I met him, in April, his eyes lit up when he told me about the plans he had for the next day. "It's my daughter's birthday tomorrow, you know. We aren't planning on doing much though. We'll all just chip in for some Chinese food. It'll be nice."

HARRY PRESTON DIED PEACEFULLY on June 13, 2019, just as this book was being prepared for printing. He was among the last of the Canadian soldiers who served Canada in the Second World War.

Harry Preston was an average soldier. He did not win any medals. He was not present on D-Day. He never shot anyone with his rifle. He was not the hero we see in movies. But he was still a hero. He answered his country's call to end Nazi tyranny. He saved lives. He saw the humanity in Germans and Canadians alike. He was the soldier without whom wars could not be fought. Harry Preston was an average soldier who went to war and was lucky enough to return home.

"To me that's the war that had to be fought," he said. "I think it's about the only war that had to be fought since. There's a reason for that war. There's no reason for the other wars, it's all just politics. Maybe I'm wrong, but I was happy to be part of it. But there's always been wars and there always will be. The next one will be a damned one."

Afterword

This book began as a classroom project in History and Writing, a third-year course I teach at the University of Toronto Mississauga. Over the years, students have told me History and Writing is the hardest course they've ever taken, but also the one most profitable to their learning. I get what they mean. It is the hardest course I've ever taught. It is also the most satisfying.

History and Writing calls on students to become intrepid reporters of historical events. They must locate primary sources and mine them to tell an original history. Some students struggle to find primary sources. Others struggle to find a story in the data. But when writers uncover a little-known aspect of the past, they can write a story that teaches about the particulars of history and directs the reader's gaze to the bigger issues.

Hammad Junejo accomplishes both in this book. Doggedly, he followed his passion for military history, in particular the Second World War, and chased his writerly instincts until he found Harry Preston, a Second World War veteran who was willing to share his story. Hammad put in the effort he needed to tell the story right. He interviewed Preston several times, consulted with experts, reviewed the literature, and more. What he produced for the class simmered with potential. After some discussion with me, he agreed to put in even more work into preparing the manuscript for publication. He rewrote, revised, researched more, then did it all a second, third, and fourth time. His efforts gave us this volume. It is a slim, succinct book with an important message. It tells us about the extraordinary life of a so-called "average soldier," the pull that war has on men, particularly young men, the power of war to bind men as surely as it destroys them, and the righteousness of the fight against Nazi totalitarianism—and any totalitarianism, in any era.

Robert Grant Price
Toronto, Ontario
April 26, 2019

Note on Sources

The information and facts mentioned throughout the story are based on my interviews with Harry Preston. Over the course of three one-hour interviews that I conducted with him from February to April 2018 at Sunnybrook Veterans Centre, he detailed his life story and his experiences during the war. I then corroborated his story with the regimental history of the 3rd Light Anti-Aircraft Regiment. The regimental history was published in Canada on a small scale shortly after the end of the war. It details the events and movements of the regiment. Not every regiment had their own history. They were written by members of the regiment, or by historical officers after the end of the war. They were likely based on war diaries and were privately published, unlike C.P. Stacey's official history. There are possibilities of some inconsistencies within the regimental histories.

I have corroborated the facts and events with scholarly sources. Most notably, I've used Stacey's official history of the Canadian Army in the Second World War. Beyond, that I've also relied on authoritative Canadian military historians and authors such as J.L. Granatstein and Desmond Morton, and Terry Copp. Two of the books I have used are special for me personally. *World War II*, by Willmott, Cross and Messenger, was the first history book I ever read when I was a child, and it sparked my interest in the war, an interest that has continued to this day and will into the future. The second book is Blizard's *The Normandy Landings D-Day: The Invasion of Europe 6 June 1944*. Both of these books helped to craft a general narrative of the war in Europe and the course of events as they occurred.

I also conducted an interview with Gregory Loughton, the Curator Emeritus at the Royal Canadian Military Institute in Toronto who was indispensable with his vast knowledge on Canadian military history. I also conducted an interview with Professor Rebecca Wittmann, chair of the history department at the University of Toronto Mississauga who, with her in-depth knowledge of the Holocaust, helped me gain a deeper understanding of Hitler's Final Solution and the Allies' response.

Bibliography

Blizard, Derek. *The Normandy Landings D-Day: The Invasion of Europe 6 June 1944*. London: Hamlyn, 1993.

Celinscak, Mark. *Distance from the Belsen Heap: Allied Forces and the Liberation of a Nazi Concentration Camp*. Toronto: University of Toronto Press, 2015.

Churchill, Winston. "The Few." *The Churchill Society*. Accessed April 13, 2019. http://www.churchill-society-lon don.org.uk/thefew.html.

---. "We Shall Fight on the Beaches." *The International Churchill Society*. Accessed April 5, 2018. https://winston churchill.org/resources/speeches/1940-the-finest-hour/ we-shall-fight-on-the-beaches/.

Copp, Terry. *No Price Too High: Canadians and the Second World War*. Toronto: McGraw-Hill Ryerson Limited, 1996.

---. *Cinderella Army: The Canadians in Northwest Europe 1944-1945*. Toronto: University of Toronto Press, 2006.

Eisenhower, Dwight D. *Crusade in Europe*. New York: Doubleday & Company, 1948.

Granatstein, J. L., and Desmond Morton. *A Nation Forged in Fire: Canadians and the Second World War 1939-1945*. Toronto: Lester & Orpen Dennys, 1989.

Hunt, Kristin. "Winston Churchill's Historic 'Fight Them on the Beaches' Speech Wasn't Heard by the Public Until After WWII." *Smithsonian.com*. November 21, 2017. Accessed February 17, 2019. https://www.smithsonianmag.com/his

tory/winston-churchills-historic-fight-them-beaches
-speech-wasnt-heard-public-until-after-wwii-180967278/.

Loughton, Gregory. E-mail message to author. February 3, 2019.

Preston, Harry. "First Interview." Interview by author. February 4, 2018.

---. "Second Interview." Interview by author. February 24, 2018.

---. "Third Interview." Interview by author. April 4, 2018.

Stacey, C. P. *The Canadian Army, 1939-1945: An Official Historical Summary*. Ottawa: Edmond Cloutier, 1948.

---. *The Victory Campaign: The Operations in North-West Europe 1944-1945. Vol. 3. Official History of the Canadian Army in the Second World War*. Ottawa: Queen's Printer and Controller of Stationery, 1960.

"The Army Show." *The Canadian Encyclopedia*. February 7, 2006. Accessed February 17, 2019. https://www.thecanadi anencyclopedia.ca/en/article/the-army-show-emc.

The History of The Third Canadian Light Anti-Aircraft Regiment from August 1940 to 7 May 1945, World War 2. Calgary: Kellaway Printing, 1955.

Toye, Richard. *The Roar of the Lion: The Untold Story of Churchill's World War II Speeches*. Oxford: Oxford University Press, 2013.

Sunnybrook Health Sciences Centre. "Veterans & Community Program." Accessed March 26, 2018. https://sunnybrook. ca/content/?page=veterans-centre-community.

Willmott, H. P., Robin Cross, and Charles Messenger. *World War II*. London: Dorling Kindersley, 2004.

Wittmann, Rebecca. Interview by author. April 4, 2019.

Acknowledgements

I'd like to thank the many people who moved this book from concept to publication.

Thanks to Harry Preston for sharing his story.

Thanks to Dr. Robert Price, without whose encouragement, support, and belief, this project would not have come to fruition. For the long conversations in his office that spawned such an idea and for his motivational speeches through trying times. For his help throughout the entire editing process and countless drafts. And lastly, for the inspiration he serves as a professor—one that I'd like to emulate someday.

Thanks to Sally Fur, who helped arrange all my meetings with Mr. Preston.

Thanks to Gregory Loughton, who supplied the introduction to this book, and without whose extensive knowledge of Canadian military history this project could not be completed.

Thanks to Sania Shahid, who accompanied me on all my interviews with Harry Preston, who patiently listened to my ramblings, and who, when I was lost, guided me with her moral support and company in better times.

Thanks to my brother and sister, Ali Junejo and Scheherezade Junejo, for their ideas, feedback, and support.

Thanks to Professor Rebecca Wittmann, who shared with me her vast knowledge of the Holocaust.

About the Author

Born in Karachi, Pakistan, in 1995, Hammad Junejo graduated from the University of Toronto with a specialist in History and a minor in Classical Civilizations. He has served as a Research Assistant in the history department at the University of Toronto, working closely with faculty to conduct focused research. In 2018/19, he interned at the Royal Canadian Military Institute, studying, cataloguing, and maintaining various artifacts, aiding in events, contributing towards exhibits, and conducting research for the curators on several military history projects.

Expressed